Who is your Mother?

Who is your Mother?

Pastor Brazz Bakka

Copyright © 2012 by Pastor Braz Bakka.

ISBN:	Hardcover	978-1-4771-5107-5
	Softcover	978-1-4771-5106-8
	Ebook	978-1-4771-5108-2

All rights reserved. No part of this book may be reproduced or transmitted in any form or by any means, electronic or mechanical, including photocopying, recording, or by any information storage and retrieval system, without permission in writing from the copyright owner.

This book was printed in the United States of America.

To order additional copies of this book, contact:
Xlibris Corporation
0-800-644-6988
www.xlibrispublishing.co.uk
Orders@xlibrispublishing.co.uk
304377

CONTENTS

Acknowledgments 7
Introduction..9

Who Is Your Mother 11
A Mother's Love 20
The Big Question Is 22
God's Love For a Kenyan mother 23
The Mother In—Law..26
My Mother...27
The Words of Wicked People that Affect Our Children 34
A Mother's Wisdom 38
The Faith of the Mother of Moses......................................40
The Window's Son (Luke 7:11-15) 42
A New Life in Him Jesus Christ 49

ACKNOWLEDGMENTS

Greetings to the Church of Shepherds Voice Ministries

May the Grace of our **Lord Jesus Christ** be with you always.

I would like to thank all those who have helped and supported me in making this publishing endeavor possible. My sincere gratitude to Lady Dee, Beverly Jura, Susan Nduati and Sylvia for their support in editing this book. I would also like to thank Lillian Ndegwa, Dacia and Michael (Birmingham) who sponsored this book. May the Lord bless you.

INTRODUCTION

How we praise God the father of our **Lord Jesus Christ**, who has blessed us with every spiritual blessing in heavenly realms because we belong to Christ.

My wife Florence Jolly and I Reverend Braz Bakka believe undoubtedly in the unfailing love and faithfulness of our **Lord Jesus Christ.**

This book is about you and me, that is;

- Who we are and where are we going
- It is important to know that man can only reproduce human life
- The Holy Spirit gives new life from heaven
- Jesus said*, "I assure you, unless you're born again, you can never see the kingdom of God."* John 3:1-3

Mothers are important and fathers but who are they?

My brothers and sisters when we speak about the nature of our mothers and fathers, we are referring to the curses from their family lineage but there is hope in Christ Jesus. This is because;

- **Jesus Christ** went on the cross and the work He did on the cross took away curses
- The work He did on the cross connected us to the blessings of Abraham through **Jesus Christ**

- Through the work He did on the cross, we receive the promised Holy Spirit through faith therefore, let us all come to **Jesus Christ** and see the real change in our lives.

1

WHO IS YOUR MOTHER

I taught art to 10-11year olds at a French primary school called **Ecolede Gaulle in Clapham.** One day, I gave them a task to draw the following:

A) A landscape
B) A fish in water.

All of them did what I asked, apart from one boy who drew a star. I asked him, "Why did you draw a star?" The young boy replied: "This is the star of David". This puzzled me and prompted me to ask him, "but why not a landscape or fish?" He said, "Mr Bakka, I love to draw the Star of David always because I am a Jew." I kept quiet and after reflecting on his answer, I realised that this boy wanted me to know who he was and that is, he was a Jew.

Who are you? You need to know who you are.

The Mother of Jesus

John 2: 1-11 (NKJV) "On the third day a wedding took place at Cana in Galilee. Jesus' mother was there, and Jesus and his disciples had also been invited to the wedding. When the wine was gone, Jesus' mother said to him, "They have no more wine." "Dear woman, why do you involve me?" Jesus replied. "My time has not yet come." His mother said to the servants, "Do whatever he tells you." Nearby stood six stone water jars, the kind used by the Jews for ceremonial washing, each holding from twenty to thirty gallon. Jesus said to the servants, "Fill the jars with water;" so they filled them to the brim. Then He told them, "Now draw some out and take it to the master of the banquet." They did so, and the master of the banquet tasted the water that had been turned into wine. He did not realize where it had come from, though the servants who had drawn the water knew. Then he called the bridegroom aside and said, "Everyone brings out the choice wine first and then the cheaper wine after the guests have had too much to drink; but you have saved the best till now." This, the first of his miraculous signs, Jesus performed at Cana in Galilee. He thus revealed His Glory, and his disciples put their faith in Him."

When you look at the power of mothers, it amazes you. Mary, the mother of Jesus proved her point that, she does have authority over her son; she led him to perform his first miracle of turning water into wine. You see, that act revealed who Jesus Christ was and his disciples believed in him.

- Get a true picture, if Mary the mother had been talking about healing that day, Jesus would have healed.
- If it was marriage, he could have done it
- If it were a financial miracle, he would also have done it.

Mothers are truly amazing, who is your mother?

Taking a deeper look I found that a lot of good things come from our mothers, but many bad things are unseen which are spiritual problems. One word was written in the book of **(Psalm chapter 51 v 5)** *I have been evil from the day I was born, from the time I was conceived I have been sinful.* I remember a man who was a professional boxer who lived in America and came back to his country in Africa. He bought a very good house for his mother but one day, something happened and an argument broke out between him and his mother. His mother got annoyed, she removed her clothes and she stood naked before her son cursing him. She then said, "You will see." I think his mother did not realise that she had put a curse upon her son. A few months later, when he returned to America, the boxer went into the ring as usual to fight. During the first round of the fight, he got hit one blow and fell down. The referee counted One, Two and Three, but the boxer did not move. The referee then touched him, the boxer was dead.

Mothers, you have to be very careful the words you speak to your children because the word contains power. Always make sure you don't speak negative words to your children, instead, whenever they are in the wrong, reprimand them without calling them names or speaking negatively in their lives because your words may come to pass later on. What I am telling you is biblical.

Let us go back to what we said earlier in the book of **Psalms 51:5** which says, *'I was evil from the day I was born'*. Let us go back to the question of being born in sin. This means, that your mother is also a product of her mother, your grandmother who is also a product of her mother, your great grandmother and the list goes on and on.

You see what follows after your conception shapes your life, some good and some evil. That is why you see that with most people; whatever things happened to their mothers happens to them. That is because you are the nature of your mother. I have seen people behaving like their mothers while some people behave exactly like their fathers. If your mother during her pregnancy was involved in witchcraft, then automatically, you are connected to witchcraft although you are not yet born. If your mother is constantly in church then she is more likely to produce a church person. These are just some of the examples of the natures that we inherit from our mothers while we are still in their wombs.

Prayer
**Our heavenly father in the name of Jesus Christ, I destroy all witchcraft from my life.
I disconnect myself from my mother's sins in Jesus Name Amen. (repeat two times)**

WHO IS YOUR MOTHER?

Many people in this world cannot ask themselves this question because of the trust and binding bond between them and their mother. Your mother is the best person in this world to honour, trust, obey and love etc. Mothers carry us in their wombs for nine months and look after us until we are grown up. It is therefore important for us to understand the work and importance of a mother.

After an in-depth look, I found that, it is not only a lot of good things which come from our mothers, but also many bad things that later affect our spiritual and physical life. The bible is very clear about this as written in **Psalm chapter 51 v 5:** *I have been evil from the day I was born; from the time I was conceived I have been sinful.*

Now say the prayer below by faith

Prayer
Heavenly Father, since I was born from my mother's womb evil has been following me. Now I declare from

the bottom of my heart, today, I disconnect myself from my mother's ancestral curses in Jesus Name.

I disconnect myself from my mother's ancestral curses in Jesus Name. I disconnect myself from my mother's ancestral curses in Jesus Name.

When you look at your life do you see your mother in you?

Some people laugh exactly like their mother, some walk like their mother, some act like their mother. If that can happen in the physical it means it can also happen in the spiritual side as well. But I am convinced that whatever negative things they did to my mother they cannot do it to me in Jesus Name.

Prayer
Every evil thing they did to my mother in the spirit and in the physical will never ever happen to me in the name of Jesus Christ. I call the names of my mother (begin to call your mother's names out) **every ceremony of evil done before I was born, I destroy it in the name of Jesus Christ.**

JOB 3: 1-4(NKJV)

After this, Job opened his mouth and cursed the day of his birth. He said: "May the day of my birth perish and the night it was said, 'A boy is born!' That day-may, it turn to darkness; may God above not care about it; may no light shine upon it."

Oh Lord God, what made him to speak such painful words in his life? Look at what he went on to say in Job **Chapter 3; 11-13** *"Why* did I not perish at birth, and die as I came from the womb? Why were there knees to receive me and breasts that I might be nursed? For now I would be lying down in peace; I would be asleep and at rest."

The suffering was too great for Job. He had lost everything. When you look closely in his speech, his mother is the subject of the argument. **Why the mother?**

WHY MY MOTHER?

The ancestral strongholds from the side of your mother are stronger than anything else in this world: You need to break down all manner of evil from your mother's side i.e. **delay, rejection, poverty, fornication, sickness etc.**

Let me tell you about a true story of two sisters' one in Africa and another one in England. Both of them are married and they have children. But, when the husband of the one who is in England refuses to sleep in the bedroom, the same thing also happens to the one in Africa. Can you see the pattern in their lives? When I asked them what they thought of this coincidence, their reply was that they thought they had inherited marital problems from their mother because the same thing had happened to their mother. Their father would often refuse to sleep in their matrimonial bed and leave their mother alone. The two sisters were now unfortunately experiencing the same marital problems as their mother. They were now sadly living the same life as that of their mother.

Your mother is a destiny maker, good bad or indifferent

To fully understand this, you need to look at the life of Rebekah, the mother of Isaac. Listen to the words of this mother. **Gen 27:11-25 (NKJV)** *Jacob said to Rebekah his mother, "But my brother Esau* is a hairy man, and I'm a man with smooth skin. What is my father touches me? I would appear to be tricking him and would bring down a curse on myself rather than a blessing." His mother said to him, "My son, let the curse fall on me. Just do what I say; go and get them for me."

So he went and got them and brought them to his mother, and she prepared some tasty food, just the way his father liked it. Then Rebekah took the best clothes of Esau her older son, which she had in the house, and put them on her younger son Jacob. She also covered his hands and the smooth part of his neck with the goatskins. Then she handed to her son Jacob the tasty food and the bread she had made. He went to his father and said, "My father." "Yes, my son," he answered. "Who is it?" Jacob said to his father, "I am Esau your firstborn. I have done as you told me. Please sit up and east some of my game so that you may give me your blessing." Isaac asked his son, "How did you find it so quickly my son?" "The Lord your God gave me success," he replied. Then Isaac said to Jacob, "Come near so I can touch you, my son, to know whether you really are my son Esau or not." Jacob went close to his father, who touched him and said, "The voice is the voice of Jacob, but the hands are the hands of Esau." He did not recognize him, for his hands were hairy like those of his brother Esau; so he blessed him "Are you really my son Esau?" he asked. "I am" he replied. Then he said, "My son, bring me some of your game meat to eat, so that I may give you my blessing."

Rebekah played a very important part in having Jacob take his brother's blessings. She is the one who plotted to have Jacob deceive his father and her plan worked. Still in all this drama, Rebekah knew that Esau hated Jacob. **Genesis 27:41 (NKJV)** *Esau held a grudge against Jacob because of the blessing his father had given him. He said to himself, "The days of mourning for my father are near; then I will kill my brother Jacob."* You see Esau, wanted to kill his brother Jacob but what Esau did not realize was that his own mother was responsible for what had happened; it was her plan that lost him his blessings to his brother Jacob.

Before I go on, I want you to read **Genesis 27: 29.** You will see between the lines, of the blessing given to Jacob that there is a statement that says, '*may your mothers' descendants bow down before you'.* Isaac knows very well that the side of your mother is where the problem is. You have dealt with the evil stronghold of your mother's side more than your father. So many people focus on curses on their father's side but they do not realise that the strongholds from their mother's side are stronger and greater. That is why Isaac said to Jacob that, 'your mother's descendants should bow down before you,' so that no power from his mother's side would stand against him.

When we look at this story closely, we realise the kind of power that Jacob's mother Rebekah had over him. When she heard about Esau's plan, she sent for Jacob and said, *"Listen, your brother Esau is planning to get even with you and kill you". Genesis 27:42*

This entire dilemma was brought on by Rebekah! Now here she goes again with another plan. My son, now do what I say. **"Go at once to my brother Laban in Haran and stay with him for a while until your brother's anger cools down and he forgets what you have done to him"**. **Genesis 27:43**

Why has Rebekah as a mother done this? Now she is indirectly saying that it's Jacob's fault. Remember very well that Jacob did not like the idea at first. His mother's lies changed the whole concept of something that should never have happened in the first place. The same thing happens even now, for example, when you plot to do something and then when things go wrong, you mention someone else's' name instead.

Ooh! Who is your mother?

When I read the story of Rebekah and her sons, it really makes me to understand that our mothers are not a joke. They play a very important role in our lives whether they are educated or not.

When the time came for Jacob to marry, Rebekah again, wanted to get involved. Rebekah said to Isaac, ***"I'm sick and tired of Esau's foreign wives, if Jacob also marries one of these Hittite women, I might as well die"***. **Genesis 27:46**

Remember Esau and Jacob were twins, here is his mother again trying to control the marriage of her son. How many times has your mother tried to control your life, marriage or even your destiny? Has it been for good motives or bad? A good mother may try to control your life because she wants the best for you but what about a wicked mother? What are her motives?

Prayer

My father in heaven, please take away the spirit of confusion sitting in my life. You evil powers that are controlling me from of my mother side, I bind and confuse you in the name of Jesus Christ, Amen. (repeat two times)

A MOTHER'S LOVE

One mother gave birth to two sons with different men, she broke up with both men but she told her sons that they were both from the same father. Faced with guilt because of her lie, she came to me and asked me what she should do about it. When I looked at her situation, it was a very sensitive matter which she had never told anyone. I said to her; "these boys are now a bit young, it will not do any good to tell them. Let them grow up to be in their thirties and then, you can tell them the truth." What do you think? It is clear that she loves both her sons and that is why she did not want to create a rift between them. She did that out of love and when the time is right, she will disclose the truth.

We really need to pray for our mothers always. Whatever they do leaves a mark on you. Every word they speak into your life will come to pass.

Prayer
Lord Jesus, please give my mother wisdom to talk to you in the name of Jesus Christ. If she is asking anything that is not good for my life destroy it in the name of Jesus Christ. Change every evil word spoken into my life. Let goodness and mercy follow me all the days of my life in Jesus Name Amen.

Some mothers control 90% of the life of their children either by prayers or by witchcraft. Recently a young mother was complaining about her mother who had destroyed her marriage. Her mother took her to a park in London at night and told her. *"You must pass under my legs three times"*. Without questioning the strange command she had been given, the young mother did exactly what she was told. A few months later, she lost her marriage and now she is looking after her two children on her own. Now, mother and daughter don't speak to each other because she later found out that what her mother told her to do was witchcraft.

THE BIG QUESTION IS

Are there any good mothers? Yes there are. Most mothers have good intentions for their child/children. Some think that when they take the names of their child/children to a witch doctor for them to become great, they are helping them. The devil has locked and destroyed many people through their mothers.

However, it should not be forgotten that, some mothers are so good they teach their children that Jesus Christ is alive and even take them to church. They nurture hope in the lives of their children and even pray with them. Such mothers make sure that their children will never forget that there is a Living God.

In the book of ***2nd Timothy 1:5***, Paul was talking to a young pastor Timothy and he said to him, *"I know you sincerely trust the Lord, for you have the faith of your mother Eunice and your grandmother Loise"*.

Try to understand this verse. *'you have the faith of your mother Eunice and your grandmother Loise"*. **Who is your grandmother?** You can connect to good and evil things from your grandmother as well. The faith of his grandmother Loise followed the young pastor and his mother Eunice as well. This shows that the good in your mother will always shine in the life or lives of her child/children.

Some people will do negative things like their mother, quarrel like their mother; some suffer problems in their marriages and rejection etc just like their mother.

By faith good things will follow, money, kindness, favour like your mother like you my dear.

GOD'S LOVE FOR A KENYAN MOTHER

In 1993 in the country of Kenya, near the city of Nairobi at a place called Kimbo, one pastor called me, I was not a pastor at the time. The pastor said to me, *"Bakka there is a mother with four children; she does not want to see anybody but she needs help and she is suffering, Mr Bakka, you go and visit her"*. The husband of this family had abandoned them. He had built a small iron sheet house for the family. I went to visit this Kikuyu woman and found her sleeping on a very rough bed breast-feeding the baby. Instead of milk there was blood was coming out, because she was very sick. She was speaking in her vernacular language and but I could not speak her language. When I entered, I called her and told her, *"I am not a Kenyan, I'm Ugandan and I have come to help you."* She looked at me sickly, her eyes were looking yellow. She then told me, *"My husband is a shoe maker in the city and hasn't come back for many months. I have decided to die"*. While she was speaking, a young boy of about 11 years, a girl of 9 years and a boy of 5 years came in. They looked at me and I greeted them. I asked them, *"Where are you coming from"*? They said, *"From a building site to beg."*

I looked at that woman and said to her, *"I am going to give you some money to go to the hospital tomorrow". We are then going to buy some food together with your children"*. I bought butter, bread and all good things for the children to eat. Then they took it home. I did not go back again. The Pastor later informed me that the woman had now recovered.

One day, while I was passing through the city market in Nairobi, I heard someone calling out to me, *"sir, sir."* I turned around and saw a woman waving at me. "Do *you remember me?"* She asked me, I said, *"no".* She said, *"I am the mother of the four children. Remember you came to see me in my iron sheet house, when I wanted to kill myself. All of us are well now. I'm now a business woman selling onions in this market".* Oh my, she looked very well. God is very kind to mothers. That is why he saved her life for the sake of her children, so that she may raise them up and live long. We really need to pray for our mothers. So that the Lord may remember them and that He may take away their pain.

Isaiah 49:15 says*: "Can a mother forget the baby at her breast and have no compassion on the child she has borne? Though she may forget, I will not forget you."*

Psalms 27: 10 says: *"Though my father and mother forsake me, the Lord will receive me."*

What a mighty God we serve. He will never forget or leave us when we call unto Him today with sincere hearts. He will make the impossible possible in the name of Jesus Christ.

HOW CAN A GROWN MAN BE BORN AGAIN?

Nicodemus asked in **John 3:5-6** *"How can an old man go back into his mother's womb and be born again a second time?"* Look Look at Jesus answer to his question; *"I am telling you the truth, no one can enter the kingdom of God without being born of water and the spirit, a person is born physically of human parents but is born spiritually of the spirit".*

- This means that you have to be baptised in water.
- The nature of your mother is in you and your father as well.

- If you allow the words of Jesus Christ to be in you and become born of the spirit you will receive spiritual understanding. **John 3:8** explains more.

We should get out from the nature of mothers and fathers and be born again. **Take on the nature of the spirit of God and not the nature of your mother.** So many people say I am like my mother or father, **change it now and take the Holy Spirit because the spirit of God is the guarantee.**

Jesus asked Nicodemus, "you are a great teacher in Israel and you don't know this?" A lot of us don't understand how this can happen but Jesus Christ is saying the truth by saying, **we speak of what we know and report what we have seen, yet none of you is willing to accept our message. Our job is willing for change and to know heavenly things.**

Will you receive and accept the good news of our Lord and Saviour Jesus Christ today? He is the only one who is able to set you free, to change your mother and the entire lineage of your family. Accept the good news and receive Him today and you will be amazed at what He will do in your life.

THE MOTHER IN—LAW

When we look at the story of Ruth and Naomi, we see that mother-in-law's also play an important role in our lives. When Ruth was determined to go with Naomi the mother in law, she said, *"Your people will be my people; your God will be my God."* **Ruth 3:1** and so she followed Naomi everywhere she went but a time came when Naomi said to Ruth, *"I must find a husband for you, so that you will have a home of your own"*. Naomi gave her daughter-in-law some very powerful instructions which altered and transformed her destiny forever.

1. *Wash yourself*
2. *Put on some perfume*
3. *Get dressed in your best clothes.*

That was good advice from a mother-in-law.

Naomi's advice to Ruth, her daughter-in-law brought a great family in this world, and changed Ruth's destiny from that of a widow and connected her to the lineage of the Messiah. Let us have a look at this family; Obed was the child of Ruth and Boaz. Obed became the father of Jesse who was the father of David. Everybody speaks of David. Jesus Christ spoke about David. Jesus Christ was called the son of David. Naomi the mother-in-law of Ruth played a very important role and all this came about because of the advice she gave to Ruth.

**Mr & Mrs Kiwanuka (Pastor Bakka's Parents)
Picture taken in 1954**

MY MOTHER

I remember time and time again, my mother would tell us not to take anything that does not belong to us. We were five boys (bothers) at that time. One day, we stole sugar and some groundnuts from the cupboard and we then agreed, if she asked, we would all deny it and say, "We have not taken anything." Our mother went into the bedroom, got some washing soap powder and put it in a big plastic bowl, poured water and mixed it vigorously with her hands until it formed some bubbles. At that particular age, we were very young and we did not know that it was soap powder until later on.

She said, *"If you refuse to talk, all of you, I am your mother and I have the power to do what I want, instead of the people of this world to kill you because of stealing, let me do it myself"*. She stepped forward and then said, *"If you have not stolen my sugar and groundnuts, when you drink from the plastic bowl you will not die"*.

Oh my! I looked at those bubbles and I knew that if I drunk it I would surely die. She insisted that I should be the first to drink it. I said, *"No"*, she told all my other brothers to do the same calling us by numbers, *"number one drink, number two drink, number three, number four, number five"*. We all began to plead with her not to kill us, begging for her mercy. We confessed that we had stolen the sugar and groundnuts and we were very sorry. She warned us very sternly, *"never touch anything again until it is given to you. Do you understand me?"* Those words have never left me to date. I still remember them as if they were said yesterday. 99% of what our mothers tell us will always remain with us forever. That is why it is very important for mothers to speak positive things in the lives of their children.

I remember one day, when we were coming from school, I was in primary school, standard four by then. I was around thirteen years. One boy called Nkabwe told me things I had never heard of before. I told him that my mother got another child from heaven and he laughed. He asked me, "which heaven?" I told him, "the real heaven!" He was running back and forth laughing at me. When he stopped running, he said to me, "Bakka children don't come from heaven. They come from your mother." Nkabwe then explained everything to me biologically and how women gave birth. I was very disappointed by what he had told me. It formed a very bad image in my mind and for a long time, I stopped sitting near my mother. In my young mind, I could not understand how my own mother would go through such a horrible act. It was because I loved her too much and did not want to think that she could have done what Nkabwe had said.

WHO IS YOUR MOTHER?

When Jesus Christ was told by his disciples that his mother and brothers were looking for Him, He replied, *"Who is my mother? Who* is *my brother"?* My mother and my brother is the one who hears the word of God and does it. Mathew 12:48-49, Then he pointed to his disciples and said, **"These are my mother and brothers and anyone who does the will of my father in heaven is my brother and sister and mother."**

Let us pray for our mothers so that they may follow Jesus Christ and not witchdoctors and evil doctrines of this world and so that we may prosper.

Many years ago, I was arrested with three other guys and we were taken to the barracks called Lubiri barracks (it is a place for soldiers). I think it is now a palace of the kingdom of Buganda, in Uganda, East Africa.

When we arrived at the barracks that was when we were told why we had been arrested. The army officer said to us, *"You have been trying to overthrow this government of Uganda"*. In most African countries, when you are suspected or even arrested and charged with trying to overthrow the government, this simply means you are now going to die. When they began to demand that we give them the guns we were hiding, I knew we were in big trouble. Every accusation they had made against us was a lie and I felt that we were going to be tortured to death. I had never even touched a gun in my life and here I was being accused of being in possession of illegal weapons. These were very ruthless soldiers who could kill you anytime and when they looked at us, fear gripped all of us, the spirit of death was hovering around us, I started praying silently.

My friend Nagib begun to call his mother, "Mother! *Mother! Mother!* We had to tell him to keep quiet. That day, we were beaten up severely but our mothers could not help us.

My prayer made a big difference because I was not beaten as much as my friends. They even hit their faces. We were then taken to another Barracks, a place where like Job, I regretted why I was ever born! They used to wait for us at the gate of the barracks with long straps made from the tail of rhinos. The army men would stand at the gate and they would beat everyone while we walked past them from the cells. No one was allowed to be left behind in the cells, you had to get out or else your legs would be brutally beaten and broken. There was no other way; you had to pass through them on your way out. While you were approaching the gate they would start beating people from every angle left and right.

I dodged the beating many times. One day, I was caught and the tail of the rhino strap went through my face, neck and chest. I felt so much pain. I thought of my mother at that particular time and wished she was there to comfort me. Mothers produce us in pain and then pain follows us in our lives. Why is there suffering in everything born of a woman? I have seen innocent people suffer. Innocent people are in prison and the wicked are out enjoying life! Why?

That is why Jesus Christ said anything produced by human is human. Pain produces pain and sin produces sin. It is only Jesus Christ who says it right. When he said to Nicodemas, "Nicodemas, *you should be born again*". Nicodemas said, **"Do I need to go back to my mother's womb?"** Jesus replied, **"No you need to be born by the spirit of God because when you're born of the spirit, no-one will understand where you are going and coming from"**.

If the mothers of this world produce pain or trouble, what did your mother produce? **Jesus said trouble will come but he also said cheer up, I have overcome the world.**

So the nature produces nature, the spirit produces spirit. I have seen many miracles but there is one particular miracle that Jesus did which amazed me. One woman came to me, *"**Pastor** I have been in marriage for 23 years, but I have no child. Enough is enough I need a child. I want to be a mother,* **Pastor** *now"*.

This woman from Zaire reminded me of Hannah, the mother of Samuel. She wanted a child so desperately, she did all she could, including giving big offerings to the Lord but she still could not get a child, She went to the temple and opened herself to God, until the servant of God called her a drunkard. Oh no, sir! She replied, I'm not drunk, **1Samuel 1:15.**

But Hannah answered and said, "No, my Lord, I am a woman of sorrowful spirit. I have drunk neither wine nor intoxicating drink, but have poured out my soul before the Lord."

This woman from Zaire said to me, *"I want to be a mother"* and I told her "yes, madam", she continued, *"I am very good in French language forgive me for my bad English when I'm talking to you"*. I asked her, *"Why don't you go to the bishop of the French church?"* "No" she said, *"It is you who can understand this"*. Then I told her, *"Go and bring a sacrifice"*. The next day she came with a sacrifice of sixty pounds. I told her, *"This is not a sacrifice"*. She looked at me and I realised that she did not understand. I then began to explain to her; *"you have been paying for IVF treatments at the hospital at £3500 per treatment and four times you have not been successful"*. Imagine she paid £3500 times for four IVF treatments that is a total of £14,000 and none of them had been fruitful. I felt her pain and humbly, I started calling her *'mum.'* I then told her, *"You go back home and bring a sacrifice please"*.

One Friday evening, she came to see me with her husband. The French speaking couple sat down and the husband asked me, *"What is a sacrifice?"* I said to him, *"wait a minute let me explain so that you understand".*

a) **Tithes:** This opens the window of heaven for you. It is like paying your taxes.
b) **Offering:** This is an investment in the kingdom of God. It is like the way people invest in mortgage, business or education.
c) **Sacrifice:** A sacrifice moves the hand of God quickly.

When I had finished explaining this to them, her husband thanked me and the couple left. The following Sunday, I believe that was back in 2007, I saw the couple walking towards the altar. The husband handed me an envelope and said, "Here is the sacrifice you said we should bring". I smiled and lifted it in the eyes of God and in the presence of the entire congregation, I said, "Heavenly Father of heaven, give them a child in Jesus name". Amazingly one year later, God blessed the couple with twins, a boy and a girl. Now she is a mother of twins. And her pain is no more

This is the Miracle that Mr and Mrs Ribeiro ... waited for twenty-three years. Doctors failed, science failed, man's knowledge failed but Jesus remember this woman and wiped away her tears.

THE WORDS OF WICKED PEOPLE THAT AFFECT OUR CHILDREN

One day a young mother left her child in a house. They were my neighbours. She went to borrow a needle and thread to sew, while she was there, an argument arose between her friend whom she had gone to see. Her friend cursed her and said, *"You will see what I will do to your child"*. So she (my neighbour) departed and decided to return back to her house. When she got back home, she looked at her son and realised that he was not breathing. She began to cry out loudly, **"My son! My son!"** I remember the man called Mutiso (another neighbour) running into the house and when he checked the boy, he was not breathing. Mutiso ran to the shops and bought some medicine called cofter. He forced the tablet into the mouth of the boy and the boy started coughing and his life came back. It was a great relief for this woman who nearly lost her son because of an evil word that had been spoken by an evil person in the heat of an argument.

Some of our mothers may not know how to protect us against wicked people and the wicked words they speak upon our lives. We need to pray for our mothers to get wisdom in Him Jesus Christ so that when wicked words are spoken, instead of them looking for a solution in witchcraft and other places, they will turn to prayers and pray for divine protection upon the lives of their children. **Mothers, I want you to know the truth, Jesus Christ is the only one who can protect your children, not charms or witchcraft. He is the only one who can keep them safe with His precious blood.**

As I mentioned earlier, the prayers of your mother can either make you or destroy you. King David in the book of Psalms 86:16 said, **"Turn to me and have mercy on me, strengthen me and save me, because I serve you, just as my mother did"**. If your mother serves God, blessing and mercy will follow you and you will see it.

THE NEGATIVE INFLUENCE OF A MOTHER

Herod had earlier ordered John's arrest and he had him chained and put in prison. He had done this because of Herodias (his brother Phillips wife). For sometime John the Baptist had told Herod. It isn't right for you to be married to Herodias! Herod wanted to kill him but he was afraid of the Jewish people. This was because they considered John to be a prophet.

On Herod's birthday, the daughter of Herodias danced in front of the whole group. Herod was so pleased that he promised her by saying *"I swear that I will give you anything you ask for"*. At her mother's suggestion she asked him (King Herod) **"give me here and now the head of John the Baptist on a dish!"**

Let us think about this mother who asked for the head of John the Baptist. If that mother is your grandmother, what about the mountain of problems she left for her daughter? If she is your mother what kind of children will she produce?

Brothers and sisters what disturbs me is that most of us, do not seem to know where we are coming from and where we are going. We should desire to be more like Timothy, to be connected to the good of our family especially our mothers and grand-mothers and disconnect ourselves from the bad or evil of our ancestors. Have a look at this; Paul thanked God as he remembered Timothy always in his prayers night and day. Paul told him **in 2Timothy Chapter 1:4-5. *"I remember your tears and I want to see you very much*** *so that I may be filled with joy. I remember the sincere faith you have, the kind of faith your grandmother Lois and your mother Eunice also had."*

Paul was connecting Timothy to the faith of his grandmother Lois and his mother Eunice! **What is in your grandmother's or mother's past?**

Isaiah 49:14-16

This is an amazing statement, when the people of Jerusalem said, *"the Lord has abandoned us! He has forgotten us!"* The Lord's replied and said; **Can a woman forget her own baby and not love the child she bore? Even if a mother should forget her child, I will never forget you Jerusalem, I can never forget you. I have written your name on the palms of my hands.**

My dear when you read this verse 49v15 (Isaiah), you will see that mothers can forget their children. **In my lifetime, I have seen mothers witching their own children!** I have told you about the lady in London whose mother told her to meet her in one of the parks at night. Her mother then said to her, *"I want you to pass under my legs three times"* and she did. Because of that she lost her marriage totally. She told me that she did not know this was witchcraft. Now they don't see or speak to each other. Our mothers are the people we respect and love but some of our mothers are the cause of the problems in our lives. You cannot choose where to be born or what mother to have but I strongly believe you can change all the negative things in your life into positives. Today, you can change your destiny through prayer and faith in Him Jesus Christ.

Prayer
The problems of my mother should never follow me
I break and confuse those curses
Father set me free in Jesus Name.
(repeat two times)

One day, I found myself in a very difficult situation. I used to teach in one of the schools in Lambeth. I was then sent to a French school in the Clapham area and while I was there teaching, the head teacher said they could not pay me unless I produced my passport which was in the home office in London. That meant that there was no pay for me. I stopped working and I was faced with so many problems. There was no more financial help for the family I had left back in Nairobi, no more school fees for my children. Things were very tight. One day during the winter, I remembered very well that I was born in sin from my mother's womb. As David said in the book of Psalms 51:5 "behold I was brought forth in iniquity and in sin, my mother conceived me." I repented my sins and left my house in Brixton and headed towards Clapham Park, it was very very cold. While I was walking, I came to a park that was full of snow. I noticed a tree and when I passed near it, it had no leaves at all. I went back and looked at that tree. I looked up to heaven and said, *"My God look at this tree, it is dried up without any leaves that is how my life is now. Please Lord, when the leaves come back on this tree, let my life come back"*. Then I remembered the book of Psalms 119:159 "See **how I love your commandments, LORD. Give back my life because of your unfailing love"**.

Let me tell you, God our LORD hears us. He heard me. Six months later, He changed my life. I found myself in a church as a pastor and I started my own meeting at **3:00 am** every day. It is still going strong eleven years later.

One day I was passing by that tree and I heard the voice of the Lord. He told me, *"look at the tree you prayed on."* I looked up and saw the leaves on the tree and I then touched my pocket. OOOH! I had money in my pocket and I am now somebody again. **Praise the Lord our God for his Love and tender Mercy towards us.**

A MOTHER'S WISDOM

I was born in Uganda and my mother was a farmer. One day as usual, she took me to the farm and put me down and left me there. She went ahead to dig. She told me because of the heat of the sun she placed me under a banana tree to dig. I was 2 years old so I couldn't go very far if I moved. While my mother was busy digging, she heard a sharp cry of my voice, then she ran toward me and saw a woman running and she shouted to her "*I have seen you, what you have done to my son God will use it for his glory!*" She looked at me and found the innocent Bakka of 2 years with cuts all over my leg. The woman who cut me had used razor blade and put witchcraft medicine or herbs in me but what my mother said came to pass, because now I serve God. What if my mother did not have the wisdom to reverse the act of that wicked woman? What if she had held me in her arms and cried all day without doing anything? What would have become of me then? Do you now see how important it is for us to pray for our mothers?

I look up to the mountain, does my help come from there? My help comes from the Lord who made the heavens and the earth.

I like this prayer

A mother in need (Matt 20:20)

The mother of James and John sons of Zebedee, came to Jesus with her sons, she knelt respectfully to ask a favour. "*What is your request?*" Jesus asked. She replied, "*In your kingdom will you let my sons sit in places of honour next to you, one on your right and the other on your left?*"

In the book of **Matthew 20:22**

Jesus told them, *"You don't know what you are asking! Are you able to drink from the bitter cup of sorrow I'm about to drink?"* **Sometimes you need a mother who understands what to ask for her children or child.** You see, this mother asked for a position which her children were not able to pay the price to be there. *"Will you drink the cup of sorrow?"* Jesus asked. **As a mother, what will you ask for your children from the Lord our God?**

THE FAITH OF THE MOTHER OF MOSES

A woman became pregnant and gave birth to a son. She saw what a beautiful baby he was and kept him hidden for three months. But when she could no longer hide him, she got a little basket made of papyrus reeds and waterproofed it with tar and pitch. She put the baby in the basket and laid it among the reeds by the edge of the Nile River. The baby's sister then stood at a distance watching to see what would happen to him.

Moses' mother was protecting her son from the orders of Pharaoh when he said all newborn babies should be thrown into the River Nile as long as they were Israelites.

Through her faith and this act, she made so many people who were in bondage to be delivered by God and rescue them from life's problem that threatened to destroy them. Moses and the children of Israel is a story of a God who loves his people so much that he rescued them from destruction.

How Can I Forget Hannah?

God can turn your life around. Let us go to the book of **1Samuel** chapter 1:5-20. Hannah's story is that of a woman who was in deep sorrow because she could not have children. A woman in those days who could not bear children was viewed as having been cursed by God. For Hannah, this infertility ended. God gave her a child whom she called Samuel, who became a mighty prophet and priest.

God turned Hannah's life around because she cried out to God for a child. The book of **1Sam 1:10-11**, tells us that God heard her cry and miraculously gave her a child. **1Sam 1:19-20** we read that the LORD remembered her. And it came to pass in the process of time that she conceived and bore a son and called his name Samuel.

For all those who think that you are cursed. Let me tell you today that in **Galatians 3:13, "Christ has redeemed us from the curse of the law"**, having become a curse for us (for it is written **"cursed is everyone who hangs on a tree")**. When you accept Jesus Christ into your life you are set free from the curses and will receive the same blessings as Abraham. **Although, being a Christian does not guarantee you a life free from trials and difficulties. You have a covenant and a right to expect God's blessings in every area of your life.**

THE WINDOW'S SON
(LUKE 7:11-15)

Jesus went to a town called Nain, accompanied by his disciples and a large crowd. Just as he approached the gate of the town, a funeral procession was taking place. The dead man was the only son of a **mother** who was a widow. When the Lord saw her, his heart was filled with pity for her, and said to her "don't cry". He walked over and touched the coffin and the men carrying it stopped. Jesus said, "Young *man! Get up*". I tell you the dead man sat up and began to talk. Jesus then gave him back to his **mother.**

Our Lord brought this young man back to life because when he saw his mother, his heart was filled with pity for her. It is the will of God for all women to be happy, to live long and raise their children while in good health. Women, you should never forget this; Jesus Loves you and wants nothing but the best for you, desire to know Him and He will do amazing things in your life.

(Mark 17:24-30)
A woman whose daughter had an evil spirit in her heard about Jesus, she came to him at once and fell at his feet. The woman was a gentile, born in the region of Phoenicia in Syria. She begged Jesus to drive the demon out of her daughter. But Jesus answered, "Let us first feed the children, it isn't right to take the children's food and throw it to the dogs. "Sir" she answered, "even dogs under the table eat the children's left over". So Jesus said to her, "because of that answer go back home, where you will find that the demon has

gone from your daughter". She went home and found the demon had gone out of her daughter.

It is good to take a step of faith believing in what you have not yet seen like this woman that is what led her to receive her miracle. She was persistent and she had faith in Jesus.

Prayer
Father in the name of Jesus Christ, help me to do what
  is right
I will not be afraid; you are my father, a miracle worker
Take my hands and lead me in the paths of righteousness
in the name of Jesus Christ Amen.

Positive power (John 2:1)

The mother of Jesus was the guest at the wedding in Canna of Galilee and when they ran out of wine, she said to him, "they have no wine." In John 2:5 His mother then said to the servants, "Whatever Jesus says, do it."

The true mother of Our Lord (Luke 1:28-33)

The angel came to her and said, *"Peace be with you! The Lord is with you and has greatly blessed you!" Mary was troubled deeply by the angel's message and wondered what the words meant. The angel said to her, "don't be afraid Mary, God has been gracious to you, you will become pregnant and give birth to a son, and he will be called the Son of the Most High God. The Lord will make him a king as his ancestor David was. He will be the king of the descendants of Jacob forever and his kingdom will never end".*

All mothers in this world need favour in the eyes of God for the sake of their children. Unless God is with you as a mother, your children or child is likely to get it rough in this world.

> **Now let us pray for our mothers. Father in Jesus Name, I pray that you touch my mother and deliver her in Jesus Name. (repeat two times)**

Who Is Your Mother?

A lot of our mothers did not seek the true God in the time when they were pregnant! Many found themselves in the hands of ancestors' traditional things like witchcraft practising, voodoo etc.

We need strong prayers against our mothers' strongholds in our lives. I have tried to show you how mothers can be influential to their children's destiny.

Now we need prayers to stop the evil done to us when we were born because some mothers give their children to the world of darkness.

POWERFUL PRAYERS ARE NEEDED DEAR BRETHREN.

(Mark 16:17) says that We were given power to perform miracles, drive out demons in the name of Jesus Christ.

> ### *Say this Prayer out loud*
> **Devil what you did to my mother you will never do it to me. Now I curse and destroy all your powers from my ancestor's side of my mother. All the powers from generation to generation from the side of my mother controlling my life I bind you in Jesus name.**

How can I get out from the nature of my mother?

1. You need to know that you're a **child of God**.
2. For every child of **God defeats** the evil in this world by trusting in Christ to give you victory.
3. Those who win this battle against the world are the ones who believe that **Jesus is the Son of God.**
4. Ask whatever you need in the name of Jesus and cover yourself with the blood of Jesus always.

    a. Is to focus on the word of God
    b. Live according to God's purpose
    c. Overcome old tradition
    d. Making the gospel relevant, don't let your tradition stop the word of God to be heard.

In the book of **Colossian 1:13-14** let us know that God has purchased our freedom with his blood and has forgiven us all our sins.

God's purpose is that we who were the first to trust in Christ should praise our glorious God.

And now you also have heard the truth. The Good news is that God saved you. And when you believe in Christ he identifies you as his own by giving you the Holy Spirit whom he promised long ago.

THE HOLY SPIRIT IS THE GUARANTEE

The Holy Spirit is God's guarantee that He will give us everything He promised and that He has purchased us to be his own people, this is just one more reason for us to praise our glorious God.

Prayer

David said in his prayer, **Psalm 142:5-7**
Then I pray to you, "O Lord I say you're all I really want in life. Hear my cry for I am very low; rescue me from my persecutors for they are too strong for me. Bring me out of prison so I can thank you. The Godly will crowd around me, for you treat me kindly".

Now, maybe your soul is in prison because of the nature of your mother or your father now cry out to God and say; *my soul get out of prison, my soul get out of sickness, my soul get out of poverty (7 times every day).*

Finally
God's spirit is the guarantee

a) Pray for the Holy Spirit to direct you
b) Being the guarantee to all good things, now ask Him for whatever you need.
c) Because the Holy spirit is the guarantee of our inheritance
d) When you look to Jesus Christ always, He will take away every evil nature from our parents and connect us to the real inheritance of God whereby there is no shame, no disappointment, because God's spirit is your guarantee.

As I conclude this book, you should know that God made all delicate, inner parts of your body and knit you together in your mother's womb. Thank God as David said in (Psalm 139:14) *"Thank-you for making me wonderfully complex! Your workmanship is marvellous and how well I know it.*

(Psalm 139:16) *you saw me before I was born. Every day of my life was recorded in your book.*

(Psalm 139:15) *you watched me as I was being formed in utter seclusion as I was woven together in the dark of my mother's womb".*

God has precious thoughts about you my friends and they are innumerable! You cannot count them they are outnumbered. This is what I am talking about and it is necessary for you to understand what Jesus Christ did for us.

In the book of 1Peter 1:18-19 before we read, I want you to be truly glad! There is wonderful joy ahead of you. The word of God says in the book of Peter that *"For you know that God paid a ransom to save you from the empty life you inherited from your ancestors and the ransom he paid was not mere gold or silver, he paid for you with the precious blood of Christ, sinless, spotless lamb of God".*

Let me tell you this, God chose Jesus Christ for His purpose long before the world began but now in these final days, He was sent to earth for all to see. And Jesus Christ did this for you.

Finally when you accept the truth of the Good-News and you trust God who raised Christ from the dead and gave Him great glory, your faith and hope can be placed confidently in God.

> **For you have been born again, your new life did not come from your earthly parents because the life they gave you will end in death but this new life will last forever because it comes from the eternal living word of GOD.** I believe Jesus Christ personally carried away our sins in his body on the cross so that we can become dead to sin and live for what is right.

Say this Prayer 3 times

I know that Jesus Christ was born, He lived, He died, He resurrected from the dead and now He is sitting on the right hand of GOD, because of that, I am saved and all the work that Jesus Christ did on the cross took away all my curses and God blessed us with the same blessing he promised Abraham, I am rich, I am blessed again and again and I receive the promised Holy Spirit through faith.

A NEW LIFE IN HIM JESUS CHRIST

1. Well, if you are born of the spirit you will become like what produced you.
2. You will see what the spirit of God sees.
3. You will be directed by the Holy Spirit.
4. You will never tell lies because you are under the voice of the Spirit of God

When you read 1Corinthians 2:9-10, God has revealed them to us by his spirit: *for the spirit searches all things, yea, and the deep things of God.*

This can help you to disconnect from your mother's nature. Read the book of **Ephesians 3:17-19**. The important point here is, when you are born of the spirit of Jesus, you will know the love of Christ for you and the knowledge of the love of Christ that surpasses all knowledge. Hagar cried for her son and the Lord answered her cry in **(Gen 21: 16-18)**. Mothers who cry for their children, always God answers them whether in sickness, misery and poverty, the Lord God Almighty answers their prayers!

I am Pastor Braz Bakka, the senior Pastor of Shepherd's Voice Ministries. I am from Uganda but I lived in Kenya for 15 years. That is where I accepted Jesus Christ as my Lord and Saviour. I was inspired and persuaded by my lovely wife Florence Jolly Bakka. When I came to England in 1995, God led me to begin night prayer meetings, which we started together with Lady Bahati from Malawi. This lasted for 7years. More than 200 people joined us and we would pray from 3:00am to 6:00am every morning. This night prayer meetings are still continuing to date and hence the meeting became known as the '3AM' service.

Pastor Bakka; "I have seen the son of the living God doing great miracles. Yes, I am still waiting to see everyone rejoicing in the unfailing love of our Lord Jesus Christ. If we are not faithful he remains faithful to us. What a Mighty God we serve." May all Glory and Honour and Power be unto the King of Kings in Jesus Name.

Edwards Brothers Malloy
Thorofare, NJ USA
April 22, 2014